LONGING

Also by Merle Feld

The Gates Are Closing
Across the Jordan
A Spiritual Life: Exploring the Heart and Jewish Tradition
Finding Words
Returning

LONGING
poems of a life

MERLE FELD

With a foreword by
RABBI RACHEL ADLER, PH.D.

CENTRAL CONFERENCE OF AMERICAN RABBIS
5783 New York 2023

Copyright © 2023 by the Central Conference of American Rabbis
All rights reserved. No portion of this book may be copied in any form for any purpose without the written permission of the Central Conference of American Rabbis.

"Shabbos together" appears in its original form in *A Spiritual Life* (SUNY Press, 1999; revised edition 2007)
"Coming of age" and "Solstice" appear in *Finding Words* (URJ Press, 2011)
Cover art: *Choosing a Path* by Asia Katz. Used by permission of the artist.

Published by Reform Judaism Publishing, a division of CCAR Press
355 Lexington Avenue, New York, NY 10017
(212) 972-3636 | info@ccarpress.org | www.ccarpress.org

LIBRARY OF CONGRESS CATALOGING-IN-PUBLICATION DATA
Names: Feld, Merle, 1947- author. | Adler, Rachel, writer of foreword.
Title: Longing : poems of a life / Merle Feld ; with a foreword by Rabbi Rachel Adler, PhD.
Description: New York : Reform Judaism Publishing, Central Conference of American Rabbis, [2023] | Summary: "In Longing: Poems of a Life, acclaimed poet Merle Feld presents a collection of deeply personal poetry reflecting on the realities of family, trauma, isolation, abuse, coming of age, love, and guarded hope"—Provided by publisher.
Identifiers: LCCN 2022034128 (print) | LCCN 2022034129 (ebook) | ISBN 9780881236262 (trade paperback) | ISBN 9780881236279 (ebook)
Subjects: LCGFT: Poetry.
Classification: LCC PJ5055.21.E425 L66 2023 (print) | LCC PJ5055.21.E425 (ebook) | DDC 892.4/17--dc23/eng/20220722
LC record available at https://lccn.loc.gov/2022034128
LC ebook record available at https://lccn.loc.gov/2022034129

Book design and composition
by Scott-Martin Kosofsky
at The Philidor Company,
Rhinebeck, NY

Printed in the United States of America
10 9 8 7 6 5 4 3 2 1

for JB

Let my people go that we may serve You

For Rabbi Sally Priesand (HUC-JIR 1972) and Lisa Feld (HCRS 2023)

Remember girdles? Remember the anger
we weren't supposed to show, or even feel?
Remember sitting and waiting to say *Bar'chu*
as someone counted, *Not one, not two . . .*
The being invisible, the tears blinked back,
fiercely. Remember the love, the innocence
assaulted, hearing for the first time, those words,

and those words, and those, such words
in a holy book, demeaning me, you, us?
All these years later, I feel the pain, rising,
constricting, afflicting. Remembering. Searching
for a reason to stay: love is stronger than death.

Tears became anger—that word—the ultimate
weapon. *She's an angry woman* (so we can
ignore her, put her down, close our ears and hearts).
Blessed be the allies, calling for the first time
from the bimah—*Taamod!* The ones who broke
through the tight circles on Simchas Torah

and passed us a scroll to hold, to dance with.
The ones who said *yes, yes, yes*. And *yes*.
And we, the wrestlers—*I won't let you go
till you bless me.* The lust, the longing, to learn,
to *leyn*, to lead, to *bensch*, to be counted, to be
called, to locate our wisdom, to inhabit our power

and our tenderness, to build holy communities,
fully and richly as ourselves, as Jewish women,
as rabbis—*I won't let you go till you bless me.*
Now, and going forward, now, and for tomorrow,

my heart soars, it flies, it bursts. From Sally to Sandy,
to Sara, from Amy and Amy to Annie, to Ariel,

Deborah, Devorah, wave after wave after wave,
I see joyous throngs—there's Rachel, and Hara, Jen,
Jamie, Jessica, Jan, and Kara. There's Sharon, and Sharon,
and Sharon! Too many to name—we're just getting started!
For so long, the world was unimaginable with you in it,

now, we cannot imagine a world without you.
We bless the work of your hands, we bless
the work of your hearts. We are blessed, to be here,
still, just at the beginning.

Contents

Foreword	xi
Rabbi Rachel Adler, PhD	
Acknowledgments	xiii
Introduction	xv

I. He is gone for many hours

In the corner	3
My brother and I each separately	4
Safe has disappeared	6
He is gone for many hours	7
Seder story	8
I keep his secrets	9
Roger is the middle child	11
I was the youngest, the only girl	12

II. Was he there, lying in wait?

Sol by the pickle barrel	15
Mickey in the hallway	17
Sixth-grade boys	20
Prospects	22
The story of how I started smoking	23
What makes you feel safe?	25

III. Ein Gedi

Shabbos together	29
Stretching infinitely	30
Red enamel chairs	31
Our demons	32
At the bottom of a colorless world	34
When you come to it, you will not care	36
Coming of age	38

IV. Lillian

The straw, day one	41
The watch, day two	42
The waiting room, day two	43
What he knew, day two	44
The dance card	45
The day the marriage ended	47
The very end of day two	49
Day three becomes day four	50

V. Temporarily, unexpectedly

When they're gone, do people know that they're remembered?	53
His many foreign lands	54
Aunt Julie's final conversation	56
What courage looks like	57
You offer me full-throated laughter	58
The pain of your loss	60

VI. Not even on the way anywhere

The story of how we came to Western Mass	65
January 9, 2017	67
Icy listserv mornings	68
Working from home	69
What's your emergency?	70

VII. Then laughed and laughed, ageless

Solstice	73
Jane is explaining	74
A bell rings	75
Under a stone	77
Respite after darkness	79
Returning	80
Stay with me a little longer please	81
The world we have longed for since the very beginning	82

Glossary	85
Index of Titles	88
About the Author	90

Foreword

Rabbi Rachel Adler, PhD

WHAT do we long for? How are our longings sustained or transmuted over the course of a lifetime? Through these haunting poems, in all their integrity, Merle Feld would maintain that longings arise out of our subjectivity, out of our individual responses to our particular life experiences.

Subjectivity has had a rather mixed reputation both in philosophy and in the social sciences. It is often portrayed as the opponent of objectivity and, hence, the opponent of verifiable truth. Yet feminists have long maintained that subjectivity presents us with another kind of truth.

In the final poem of this collection, entitled "The world we have longed for since the very beginning," Feld rejects the question "When do you feel safe?" She concludes, "That question is too small for me—":

> it's not about my safety. I climb over my fears, they are not interesting.
> I break rules, create rules—here cruelty is forbidden, here we trust,
> respect, protect one another from harm. Here together we dare to make
> the world we want to share, the world we have longed for
> since the very beginning.

Our stances toward the world as we experienced it in childhood, Feld asserts, can be transformed when we seize power ourselves and use it to make the rules and construct the world we longed for. If, like Feld, we were abused or terrorized as children, if we bore a constellation of stigmatized identities (in Feld's case, being female and being poor), rather than remaining enslaved by our traumatic histories, we can remake the world.

The received wisdom would have it that remaking the world cannot be an individual project; rather, it needs to be cooperative and communal. Feld, however, seems to have it both ways: sometimes she singlehandedly embodies vision; sometimes she draws others into her vision, creating community along the road. Either way, this is an enterprise that Feld engages in on behalf of others as much as on her own behalf:

committing to teaching adult learners in a community college setting, those whom our society often does not treat with respect; facilitating Israeli-Palestinian dialogue on the West Bank during the first intifada, bringing focus and open-hearted attention to the wounded; sitting one-on-one with a rabbinical student or seasoned rabbi, listening for the cry of the soul, the struggle toward authenticity; making truthful and unflinching poetry and two impactful plays. In America, in Israel, and across the former Soviet Union, she joins with other Jewish feminists in our mission to reenvision and inhabit a world in which patriarchy has been transcended.

Merle Feld is a truthful poet, and I mean by that all that we mean by truth in Hebrew. The root *emet*, "truth," is conjoined with a closely related Hebrew root, *amen*, which is associated with faithfulness and trust (*emunah*) and, interestingly, skill and art. Art is *omanut*, and a skilled artisan is an *omen* or *omenet*. Etymologists say that the two roots *alef-mem-nun* and *alef-mem-tav* were once the same root. This suggests that "truth" expresses for the Hebrew mind an integrity that is lived out in human doing and making, rather than being an abstract, disembodied value, as Western philosophy understands it. When I read Merle Feld's poetry, I am awed by her *emet ve-emunah*: the alchemy with which she transforms pain and struggle into beauty and laughter, galvanizing truths and tender compassion, and infuses the transmuted elements into individual and communal lives.

> *Rabbi Rachel Adler, PhD, the Rabbi David Ellenson Professor Emerita at Hebrew Union College–Jewish Institute of Religion in Los Angeles, was one of the first to integrate feminist perspectives into the interpretation of Jewish texts and law. Her book* Engendering Judaism: An Inclusive Theology and Ethics *(1998) was the first by a female theologian to win a National Jewish Book Award for Jewish Thought. She has published over sixty-five articles on Jewish thought, law, and gender, as well as the whimsical* Tales of the Holy Mysticat, *a prizewinning resource for adult education. She holds a doctorate in religion and social ethics from the University of Southern California and rabbinic ordination from HUC-JIR.*

Acknowledgments

I BEGIN with appreciation for Rabbi Hara Person, chief executive of the CCAR, for her generous encouragement of my work through the years; and for Rafael Chaiken, director of CCAR Press, a truly kind and patient man, who understands poetry and poets. Their discernment and support, their wise minds and hearts, have allowed you, my readers, to now come to know these poems, savor their rhythms, and mull over their meanings. Thanks also to copy editor Debra Hirsch Corman and proofreader Michelle Kwitkin for their commitment to excellence.

Gail Reimer and Sharon Dunn have accompanied me through many years, as beloved friends and first readers; they've taught me whatever I know about applying form and craft to initial sparks of inspiration.

I am deeply grateful to Rachel Adler, for her spiritual companionship and for articulating what is at the heart of this book; to Bulgarian-born Israeli artist Asia Katz, whose painting so perfectly provides the cover art; and to my dear friend, designer Scott-Martin Kosofsky, for his abundant professional mastery.

In many ways, this is a book about resilience, a gift I think I received most of all from my mother's mother, Bertha Uhrbach, who, not yet sixteen in 1896, traveled alone across an ocean to a New World and then supported herself by day sewing in a sweatshop and by night on her hands and knees, scrubbing the floors of the new and grand Brooklyn Academy of Music. Miraculous, your insistence, Bertha, on "choosing life." Generations later, your great-grandchildren, among them Lisa and Uri Feld, continue your quest to choose life in a new world.

I owe much to my brother Warren, from the earliest years when he gave me my allowance to most recently in that he allowed me to share the stories of our childhood in these poems.

Barely out of my teens, falling in love with Eddie Feld but terrified of making a commitment, I was reassured by our friend of blessed memory David Goodblatt: "Whatever else, Merle, if you marry Eddie, you'll never be bored." Boredom, no; rather, blessings beyond measure to be respected, encouraged, cherished, to have had a life partner who saw and helped bring forth my best self. Eddie is also a sensitive and astute reader of poetry, whose attention has enhanced many of these poems.

Most difficult of all is to try to adequately express what I feel about the person who accompanied me as I retrieved and then sat with the memories contained in these pages. Buried for decades, memories that mysteriously, repeatedly subtracted, diminished, disconnected me from the simple daily joys of my adult life. Abuse and trauma allow you only shallow in-breaths of happiness, all the more puzzling when your present existence is filled with light and love. Light and love achingly out of reach on many or most days. Every day now, JB, my heart swells with the pleasures that are mine. I am finally able to breathe them in fully, deeply. My gratitude forever that you helped me walk the treacherous path that leads to joy.

Introduction

I ARRIVED in Princeton as a young wife in my mid-twenties and left nineteen years later, the mother of two, ages nine and thirteen, launched in my work as poet, playwright, activist. For all that time, I saw the same skilled, affable ob-gyn, Fraser Lewis, who, as I gradually learned, served many of the women of the university—he was himself a Princeton grad and earned the loyalty of the then-few female faculty and administrators and the many wives of such. I bemusedly recall lying on his table, year after year, feet in stirrups, as he engaged me in conversation. It was always the same, the baritone—"How's Ed?" ("Ed," my husband, was rabbi to the university community.) Did I ever interrogate the strange, some would say ludicrous, disjunction of being both invisible and intimately seen? Through the years the generous gloss I chose to put on it was that he imagined this topic of conversation—my husband—relaxed me, made me more comfortable, or that it made him more comfortable as he explored the privacy of another man's wife. Certainly, its inevitability was a source of amusement for me.

Eddie and I eventually moved to the Upper West Side when he was chosen as rabbi of a synagogue with a venerable history. For the next four years, I regularly revisited the small university town (which I lovingly referred to as "Anatevka"), reconnecting with numerous deeply cherished friends who had come to constitute home for me. I typically drove but sometimes took the train, the last leg from Princeton Junction to Princeton proper on the charming two-car "dinghy," as it was called. One such time, as I was getting off at the Princeton station, I suddenly saw Fraser Lewis waiting to take the dinghy for the reverse trip. We smiled with delight at one another, but I was truly stunned by his greeting: "So, are you famous yet?" In all the years on the table I couldn't recall his ever inquiring about my work or artistic life, ever betraying any knowledge thereof. In a nanosecond, I remembered my childhood dreams of seeing my name on a Broadway marquee, my fantasies of being a celebrated "authoress" (as we called them when I was a child). I responded, with a wistful smile, "No," and was touched to see his face fall on my behalf. Then, I rethought the truth of that—poetry, plays, well-known prayers of mine—and amended my pronouncement: "Well, I guess I am famous in the Jewish world." He lit up with great satisfaction, broadly grinned, and boarded the little train.

In some ways, this story presages many of the poems you are about to read in the first two sections of this book, "He is gone for many hours" and "Was he there, lying in wait?" What is it to be invisible, to be invisible as a young child, a girl? What is the cost of invisibility? And then, what renders you visible? To others, to yourself? What are the costs of visibility for those who are female-presenting? How have I been shaped—bent?—as a person inadequately protected, trapped in the conflicted irony of invisibility/visibility?

This collection of poems also opens the question of what constitutes home. What do we need to feel at home, as children, as adults? (How could I, for instance, a Jewish girl from Brooklyn who grew up wearing hand-me-downs, have come to feel at home living in a town like Princeton, bastion of privilege and wealth, comfort zone of the WASP upper classes?) Remarkable and primal, the ongoing longing for *shalom* and *sh'leimut*, peace and wholeness, the safety of home. An ongoing wonder, not a small miracle, how we come to establish home, first and foremost a home that embraces, nourishes us, offers us safety, and then opens the door to others, in ever-widening circles.

I tell a story in *A Spiritual Life* (SUNY Press, revised 2007) of going to get a new driver's license as the stay-at-home mother of little children, a woman who cooked and baked each week to welcome numerous Princeton undergraduates to our Friday night table. The DMV form called for "occupation," and what I really wanted to write was, "I make Shabbos." I was, and have always been, a homemaker, even as my little children grew, even as I went from unpublished to published, even as I traveled to faraway places to share my poetry, to embody my activism, often to do both at once. An unabating hunger for home pulsed within me. Just as I had once shared my Friday night table to provide sweetness and safety to young college students and other wandering seekers, I have opened my heart to the rabbinical students and now the rabbis I mentor through a spiritual writing practice. The impulse is born in the same place: having honed the capacity to create home—whether in a physical space with roof and windows or an emotional space of warmth, caring, and listening—it feels to me only natural to share that home with others.

Intricately interwoven with the question of "home" is a related question: To whom and how and why do we attach ourselves to others, beginning with a parent, a caregiver, an intimate family circle? This collection, above all, unflinchingly examines those familial attachments and disruptions. The poems explore the experiences and ties by which we are bound to the myriad of those who make some essential part of life's journey with us; they consider what unfolds when we find the courage to trust, to open and meet one another fully in the moment, and to offer one another the truth of our existence. In this I am surely a Buberian, experiencing every connection as potentially both holy and healing. As these poems face questions of attachment, they also face questions of disruption and violence, and then the question of ultimate disruption: How do we survive the inevitable pain of loss?

While I prize a good laugh and savor whimsy when it comes to me in my writing as a gift, I must admit that many of the poems in this book are not easy. Though straightforward in literal meaning, some are difficult, painful, violent, perhaps shocking to read, especially some of my childhood and adolescent experiences. (There is no "fiction" in these poems—I save invention for my playwriting.)

An unanticipated afternoon many years ago thrust me back into old, deeply repressed memories of violence. I was at a five-day retreat with an extraordinary community of Jewish feminists, B'not Esh, who have come together year after year to explore questions of meaning, creativity, activism, and the feminist transformation of Judaism. I no longer remember what the session was that afternoon, just that we sat together in what we later referred to as "the piano room" and one by one, amidst terrible sobbing, well over half of us began describing the domestic violence we had endured in childhood. I found myself sharing stories of my own, stories that lay buried deep in my soul, suddenly erupting to the surface. Wary of "false memories," I described them to my brother, ten years older than I, when I returned home. And he said, yes, that's all quite true, accurate.

If we've been subject to violence, it may remain for most of us unexamined, closeted. My decision in this collection has been to open the closet, to expose old pain and festering wounds to fresh air as part of the process of healing. With courageous and loving companionship, such exploration can finally give us some control—we can rise up from being the victim, claiming our own strength and resilience and begin finding meaning, direction, and commitment to different ways of being. Seeing ourselves in this new light, we can tame suffering, hopefully short-circuit the cycle of suffering.

It has seemed to me natural, fruitful, to contemplate the story of how we become who we are, what struggles have been seeded in us from the beginning, how we have grown from them into our future potential for deeper understanding, greater purpose, and meaning-making. A companion challenge to the experience of visibility/invisibility is the question of how we establish an identity, most especially when there is no adequate mirror in which to see ourselves. The search for self—the reliable self, the authentic self, the truest self, even to acknowledge a beautiful self—these are quests that weave in and out through the poems included here.

I came to know myself first as a writer. Lacking someone who was truly listening, I began to find comfort, possibility, a path to release and self-recognition in conversations with myself on the page. And what was more delicious than the play with words?

Then, as a teen, I claimed firm ground within my Jewish self: I was drawn in by the warmth and shared respect I experienced in community, by prophetic visions and activist fervor, by the earnest search for meaning, the concomitant study and love of words. As in my previous books, some of the poems in this volume are explicitly Jewish, others perhaps more elusively so, more broadly spiritual—for me the borders between those two realms are permeable. I include here poems set at the Shabbos table, in the shivah house, poems whose imagery harkens back to biblical texts, Chasidic wisdom, Yiddish literature, poems born and breathed into being as prayer. Equally, there are poems revisiting the miracle and reality of childbirth; recalling memories of raking leaves and reaching for hope; standing in awe of the Oriental red poppies that return every spring to my little front yard garden; asserting self-worth against all odds; and most especially, poems that notice, uplift, and rejoice in the connection between one lonely soul and another. Don't we all contain a lonely soul within us, yearning, longing?

It would be impossible to imagine how I claimed my voice without coming of age alongside second-wave feminism, shoulder to shoulder with other women who like me woke up to the limitations imposed on us, questioning and resisting the pressure to be not-quite-so smart, thoughtful, outspoken, insistent, demanding, accomplished, assertive, strong-willed, radical . . . above all, uncomfortably unfeminine. We empowered each other, supported by men who took no pleasure in women being "less than" and who chafed as well against sexist hierarchy. Over these decades, we came to take our victories for granted. It would seem that we can no longer continue to do so, as courts low and high roll back the legal victories we fought for and won.

Another essential question calls to be addressed: Why do I write? I write to be myself, to know myself, to keep trying to know myself, to understand, to free pain and release it; to comfort myself and to visit with my own lonely soul. And why do I send what I write out to the world? I've heard from those dear to me and from strangers alike that they have felt moved, comforted, graced by my words. All of us as readers are indebted to the courageous ones who lift the veils of human experience and say, "This is my truth; let's speak truth to one another and see how it changes the world."

Over and over throughout the years, at readings, retreats, scholar-in-residence weekends, and gatherings where I have seen myself as an anonymous participant, people approach and begin by confiding, "I don't usually read/like poetry, but . . ." and then launch into how this poem or that brought tears of recognition, adding, "How could you possibly have gotten inside my mind or heart to speak the words that are mine?!"

I envision you, my readers, younger and older, as also yearning for self-understanding, yearning to articulate deeply felt mysterious truths, feeling the impulse to follow the breadcrumbs as I do, to make meaning of life's confusion, tragedy, and unexpected moments of blessing and peace. Like most writers, I address multiple audiences, distinct yet overlapping: Jewish readers and all readers who seek the sacred; feminists reaching for the fullest lives imaginable; parents raising girls and boys and nonbinary children who look everywhere for any possible wisdom across a gamut of almost limitless questions; people who grew up with scarce advantages, who needed to make their own way, and those privileged with opportunity, trying to understand a wider view of human experience; people who love freely and generously and those who struggle with shyness, uncertainty, and the courage to be who they are in the world; those who have loved—a parent, a sibling, a companion, once-in-a-lifetime friends, teachers—and those of us who've lost them. Sooner or later, that's all of us.

I continue through the years to interrogate myself: What is a worthy life? Etched in my mind is an iconic image of Rabbi Abraham Joshua Heschel, arm in arm with civil rights leaders of the 1960s, marching to Selma with Dr. Martin Luther King Jr. The image is of a man with white hair, white beard, an old man. But in fact, Heschel died at sixty-five, an age I view now through the rearview mirror. So while I feel challenged by his self-description as "praying with his feet," the truth is that, riffing off the wonderful witticism about Mozart, if I were Heschel, I would be dead now. In reality, my body no longer carries me full steam ahead to do so many of the things I'd like to do, to realize visions I still have, and in this particular context, to be the activist I was in years gone by. And I feel the modern-day prophet Heschel accusing me: Are you still living a worthy life? Do you deserve to silence guilt that you no longer pray with your feet, can no longer pray with your feet?

My generation, the baby boomers, need once again, as we always have, to reinvent ourselves, to redefine our activism, to assess yet again what today's needs are and how we can help. Many I know are responding to these questions by volunteering locally; praying with our checkbooks and laptops; organizing across the country and around the world while sitting at home; studying new issues with which we are unfamiliar; teaching what we've learned; and, not so long ago, making masks galore when that seemed the need. As grandparents, we respond with "babysitting"—an inadequate and trivializing catchall for providing care, love, safety, and foundation for the next generation.

As for me, the days of facilitating dialogue on the West Bank are long gone, as are the summers at Seeds of Peace and the time I spent in Ukraine almost twenty years ago—an unlikely three-week book tour introducing the Russian-language version of *A Spiritual Life*. There I crisscrossed the countryside, visited cities large and small, engaging in soulful conversations about myriad poems and life experiences across multiple generations from university students to the aging poor to mothers and grandmothers in Rosh Chodesh groups. The days of activating body, mind, spirit—all engines firing at full force—were a blessing.

As those days of praying with my feet began to slow down, I moved into a new role, creating spiritual writing groups for students attending rabbinical schools across all denominations. Beginning in 2004, I regularly commuted from Western Massachusetts to New York, Boston, and Philadelphia, group work morphing to focus on developing intense one-on-one relationships, providing guidance, mentoring, support, and safety for future rabbis and cantors. I encouraged them to reflect, to locate and develop a true, authentic voice, and to find the courage to be themselves and thus to grow, to soar. Work with rabbinical students evolved into work with rabbis, the commuting shifting to phone or Zoom as my mentees moved to posts across the country and abroad. In every session, I endeavor to welcome them into their own holiness and possibility.

I channel my energy into mentoring, supporting those in younger generations who are giving their all serving others. Sometimes now that means providing an island of safety for them to question, despair, recenter; sometimes strategizing about how they can best help the congregants, students, and nonprofits they serve. It is perhaps as simple as offering a way station to rest for a short time the feet that ache from praying. I've needed to rethink, "How can I be of help?" and to continue reformulating that as I, my body, and the world change. I never expected to be blessed with such a large life, such meaningful, joyful work.

I am honored and rejoice that CCAR Press has welcomed me, providing a home for my words. My hope is that these poems will find their way to you, to all who are longing and seeking connection.

MERLE FELD
Northampton, Massachusetts

I

He is gone for many hours

In the corner

I see myself sitting on a small chair
in the corner. I can't see if I am
looking at a picture book or doing
something with my hands. Perhaps
not doing, just being. Small children,
at least in those days, were allowed
that. Actually, even today, the relief,
agony, danger—being invisible.

I think I am very quiet, still. I am
taking it in—the sounds, the large
people in the room. Sometimes,
in that corner, I am peaceful,
absorbing my mother's presence,
her aura. Storing it up for when
she disappears—like when the sun
disappears behind a cloud.

My brother and I each separately

Where am I when the large man
beats the gawky adolescent boy?
I do not see, I am not in the bedroom
where my parents sleep when my father
says, *Pull down your pants*, when
my brother pleads, *No. Why? No.
What have I done? No. Please.*

My brother and I each separately
struggle to make sense of this,
but it has no reason, at least none
attached to the boy. The large man
is angry, he needs to beat someone,
and the adolescent boy is the one.
I hear my brother pleading
as I hear my father remove the strap

from his pants. He demands, *Bend over.
I'm not going to ask you again.* Why
does the boy bend over? He is a good boy,
obedient, though he is still pleading,
begging. I can almost see him
through the wall with his pants
around his ankles, bent over as instructed,
his bare flesh exposed. Then

the sounds of the strap on his flesh,
the sounds of his screaming, the sounds
of his pain, the sounds of his crying.
I am afraid, hiding in a corner.
Each time I hear the sound of the strap
on his flesh, the screams, the sobbing,

I imagine my brother's pain.
The years pass. I am three, four, five, six.

I say nothing.

Safe has disappeared

Each time after the beating I try
to reestablish normal. We are all
in a daze, not able to believe
what has happened in our home,
struggling to rebuild safe,

but safe has disappeared, it cannot
be reestablished. Still, I try, I reason—
what caused the fury, the anger,
what happened right before, how
can we avoid the before next time?

I become a lookout, a watchman,
a diviner of moods—the glint
in an eye, the beginning of a grimace
on the lips, a large body that
suddenly becomes rigidly disapproving.

I see I am without girlish charms,
I see I am unable to distract him.
I cannot execute a sweet feminine
twirl that then brings a smile, that
relaxes, tames, the crouching beast.

I am vigilant, but without power.

He is gone for many hours

When he is beaten, he makes
animal sounds. When the man
is done, the adolescent gets up
and leaves the apartment. He is gone

for many hours. My mother says
nothing, but I read the fear
in her eyes—*this time he will
not come home. I may never*

see him again. Finally though,
long after the sun has set,
I hear his key in the lock.
He has waited till everyone

is going to bed. He says
nothing. He takes his sheets,
his pillow, from the closet,
makes up his bed on the couch

where he sleeps. Lights out.
Wafting through the door,
sounds from the living room,
late night comics on TV.

Seder story

I am a simple child with many questions.
My father is out of work. He puts on his suit
and disappears into the city every morning
pretending to be like the other fathers.

Sometimes I come home in the afternoon,
startled to find him, staring dumbly at the television.
I sleep in the bed that belonged to the first son—
now that I am too big for my crib, he

must sleep on the couch. What if he wants
his bed back, reclaims his bed? My brother
the second son disappears into baseball,
tennis, basketball. He always seems fine.

I wonder why I can't be fine like he is.
Our family has no fourth child, they prayed
it would be so. The fourth child has no body,
and so no questions.

This night will be like all the others.

I keep his secrets

Late afternoon, my mother and I, in the foyer of the tiny apartment.
At the table where sports statistics pass for supper conversation,
covering the pain that throbs just underneath. Now at dusk,
I am engrossed in my homework. I love junior high school. I
have a crush on most of my teachers, but especially the ones
who introduce me to *Great Expectations* and *O Pioneers*, the ones
with whom I share serious conversations about ideas and feelings.
Especially the men, young, alive, piquing my curiosity, listening,
enjoying me, their eyes shining with wonder when I speak in class.

My mother is here with me, after a day of first graders—finally
promoted to "permanent sub." Teaching, shopping, errands, laundry,
starting dinner, now, with me, in the foyer, ironing. Just the two of us,
peaceful. At the end, she always leaves me his handkerchiefs
to practice on. And then, in his hat, his expensive business suit—
he likes to treat himself—with a briefcase and the evening paper
under his arm, he comes through the door. Is she nervous? She says,
You're home early, how was your day? And he says, *I got fired.*

Just like that. And I am falling falling falling . . . the ground
has opened under me and I am falling falling falling falling . . .
like a Disney Alice in Wonderland, in her blue dress and white
apron, falling falling falling falling. . . This is not the first time.
Like the other times—I know the drill, no need to say it—*don't tell.
Anyone.* This time though. This time when I am finally finished
falling, like Alice, I am in a new world. At last, clarity—
in this world, the earnest prayers of children are truly unheard.

In this world, it is irrevocably officially verified—I am invisible,
I actually do not exist. No need to shelter me, no need
to take his wife into another room and then later have her break
the news more gently to me, their child. Invisible, I do not merit

the protection one normally affords children. He does not see
my world has shattered, my irrepressible childish longing—
for normal, for safe—it is now finished. All that matters about me
is that I do not tell what I have heard, what I have seen.

What matters about me is that I keep his secrets.

Roger is the middle child

Somehow he is the favorite,
he is the one on whom my father
has pinned all his hopes. He has
"regular features," he looks most
"American," a regular guy.
He is self-confident, a ready smile,

not threatening, not questioning.
He has learned, taught himself
to disappear, become invisible
when trouble is brewing. He does not
hear, or notice. He sees nothing
untoward.

When we three are sitting shivah,
of course we tell stories. Mostly
the stories that make us laugh.
But also, we begin to speak
of the horrors, hidden away
for decades in dark corners.

Warren tells a story, and though
there are ten years between us,
I recall, concur, add another detail.
Roger, the middle child, *I don't
remember that.* Then I share a story
and Warren validates. But Roger says,

I don't remember that. And on it goes.
Finally, Warren, wryly, *Are you sure
you were part of this family?*

We love each other. Together we laugh.

I was the youngest, the only girl

I learned I was a coward at such an early age
when I would pull the covers over my head
conjuring music and words to familiar show tunes
while my father, one thin wall away, red-faced,
removed the leather belt from his trousers
and demanded in a cold even tone that my brother
pull his pants down and lean across the bed.

My brother, then 13, 14, 15, 16, would repeatedly
plead in a child's voice, *no please no please*
all the while obediently doing as he was told.
And then, from the next room, sounds of the strap
on my brother's flesh, the animal whimpers and cries
that followed each lash until my father's anger
was spent.

Underneath every sin I have sinned in all the decades
since, a steady daily progression decade by decade
of common ordinary sins, no more or less in number
or essence than any other ordinary woman or man,
underneath all those ordinary adult sins is the oft-
committed single sin that sets me apart from common
decent humanity, from the family of man. What sets me

apart is the single first sin repeated again and again.
That I never put myself in the doorway of my parents'
bedroom, planted myself in the doorway with set jaw,
tight lips, met my father's fury with my own determined
fury and declared, *You'll have to go through me this time.*
Instead I lay in my bed, shivering, under cover,
soaking in the animal cries, secretly grateful to be

a small child, a girl, unworthy of notice.

II

Was he there, lying in wait?

Sol by the pickle barrel

Sol presides over the pickle barrel
and the dairy case like a sloppy guard
at Buckingham Palace. His uniform,
a full white apron, not dirty, but not

clean. The dairy section and the pickles
are at the rear of the small corner store
and I am proud when I am deemed old
enough to go by myself with a list

and some money to do a bit of shopping
for my mother. Sometimes it's a list
and sometimes I just walk the two blocks
softly repeating under my breath,

*milk, sour cream, American cheese, milk,
sour cream, American cheese,* holding
tightly to my mother's small change purse.
I'm so proud I've been deemed old enough.

As I pass Sol at the back of the store
to reach the dairy case, I feel a large hand
on my bottom. I am very confused—
why is he touching me? I don't like this.

I am so confused. The hand lingers as I try
to get by him. I want to cry now, to cry,
to cry out, but I can't cry out—
it would call attention to me, and I,

I am shy, I don't want strange eyes on me.
Next time it is the same. At home I plot
how I might get past him and his large
hand, but though he's heavy and dull,

he's agile with the hand and there's
no way past him. I can't tell my mother
about his hand, I just begin to bob
and weave when she asks me to shop for her.

The simple joy of being deemed old enough has evaporated.

Mickey in the hallway

I couldn't predict
when Mickey
would be lying in wait
in the dark narrow
hallway that led to
my ground floor apartment
at the back of the building.

Bigger than me, older
than me, old enough
for urges, old enough
to mark me, to notice
I had started to develop
two buds on my chest.
He'd press

his chunky body
up against me,
grope with his hands,
try to pin me down
with his mouth.
Me, moving my head
back and forth

rapidly, desperately,
to avoid his mouth.
Of course, he meant
no harm—he was
a neighbor, upstairs,
Roger's friend, they
played stickball together.

Sometimes
on rainy days, we three

played Monopoly.
He was just doing
what boys do, and I,
too frightened,
too embarrassed,

to fill my lungs
and scream. I fought
as best I could,
pushing with my fists.
He relied on
my discretion.
All unremarkable

really, in those days,
back then,
to be expected,
in those days.
But most especially,
at the end of the day,
coming home, knowing

supper would soon
be on the table,
electric fear
coursing
through my body,
in my tightened
belly, as I opened

the heavy outside
door to the building,
my eyes darting

down the dark
narrow hallway,
my apartment door
at the other end,

was he there,
in the hallway,
lying in
wait?

Sixth-grade boys

Probably most of us started needing
or wearing bras by sixth grade.
(I heard later that girls who didn't
yet need a bra eventually wore one anyway,
embarrassed to be left behind.)

And then of course, the gauntlet of boys—
putting hands on the back of your blouse
and feeling for the strap. Once located,
they snatched it with their fingers
and snapped and laughed.

My goodness, where was that memory
stored, and what beckoned it forth?
What did I feel then? they were obnoxious?
boys will be boys? boys are obnoxious?
It stung a little—the metal hooks and eyes

hitting your bare skin with some force.
That was a small detail though, hardly
consequential. So what was the sting?
Today, carefully reflecting, I realize
not all the boys snatched and snapped—

not Alan Suntup who competed with me
for best in math—he fought fair, saw me
on the playing field, a worthy opponent.
No, it was Sherman mostly, he led the pack.
Looking back, I see clearly how he resented me,

with my 100s on tests, relentlessly waving
my hand in the air. Finally, in sixth grade,

he could find a way with his fingers, to put me
in my place, to snatch and snap and say,
Hah! Hah! Hah! Hah! Hah! You're just a girl!

Prospects

J, 16, was a redhead, golden really, like Robert Redford.
I was 13 or so when we stood together under a rose arbor
at the Brooklyn Botanic Children's Garden, when he gave
me the lightest of kisses at the end of the summer.
I floated in the memory of that kiss for a long time.

S, also a redhead, carried my books, walking me
to the bus stop after classes at Erasmus. I patiently
would explain I didn't feel "that way" about him
and then every six months I'd reluctantly agree
to go on a date. The Circle Line Cruise around

Manhattan, a Broadway show—*She Loves Me.*
F at Brooklyn College had a red convertible in which
we spent a lot of time. L took me to see Peter, Paul
and Mary at Carnegie Hall. I pined for Y, a redhead too,
pined and pined. G was the dull brother of a friend.

Where is she going with this you want to know?
Most Saturday nights I sat at home, alone, watching
TV in the family circle, hope waxing and waning,
actually, unsure, what could be hoped for.

The story of how I started smoking

I misunderstood Billy's eyes—small,
narrow, the way they tracked me.
Nineteen, too old for this to be my first time
away from home. Home, a bitterly deceptive
word for where I lived. Desperate not to be
there anymore. Instead, here in the country,
at camp, a counselor in the Catskills.

His eyes—I thought it meant he saw me—
also a first. Billy was in charge, the director.
That first week, just the counselors, he lectured—
child psychology, adolescence. I listened, took
careful notes, his eyes tracking me, noting,
I imagined, my intelligent questions. I was an
excellent student, enjoyed learning new things.

A night that first week, before kids and duffel bags,
we went for a walk on a dark country road,
lit by the stars and the glowing ember of his cigarette.
I opened my heart, I told him everything. Well,
not about the beatings and the ever-present fear—
all that too deeply buried for any words yet. But
I did tell the stories of watching, tracking,

my father's descent into darkness, expressionless
at last, no energy left for anger. My pain undammed,
pouring out, shaking, and the tears.
Billy took me back to his cabin, lay me sobbing
and open on his bed, and then he got on top of me.
For the first time in my life, I filled my lungs
and screamed, filled the air with my screams.

People came running. I can still see him, pale,
afraid, his back against the wall, explaining—

She was hysterical, I was trying to comfort her.
Quick thinking, Billy was well practiced.
Someone took me—to the cot in my bunk?
the cot in hers? I remember nothing. I had no words.
The next morning, kids and duffle bags, and so began

my summer. Away from home, unthinkable to go
back. Instead I did what I always did—shoulder
to the wheel, I'm not really here, what needs
to be done today. And every day, the whole summer
long: flag raising, announcements, breakfast,
lunch and supper, on the boat dock, color war, he was
there. And at night, walking the dark country roads,

lit by the glowing ember of his cigarette, Billy at bay.

What makes you feel safe?

I'm sitting with a woman who is learning
to be a rabbi—she is one of my students—
and I give her a prompt, *After Pittsburgh,
what makes you feel safe?* I watch

as she writes—breathing deep, then softly
repeatedly sighing to herself as words flow
from her pen. The prompt was a risk, I'm relieved
she has found a way in. Though I often write too,

this morning I have taken refuge in watching,
describing her. But Merle, come on—you want
them to be courageous—what do you say?
Because your father looked right through you,

refused you refuge or solace in his arms, his lap,
because he could turn without reason or warning
from smooth charmer to obliterating force as you
held your breath, waiting for his next explosion,

is that reason for you not to feel safe? Is Billy
with a cigarette still lurking on a dark country road?
Mickey waiting in the hallway on Crown Street?
Do you still cling to those things, pathetic excuses?

Please, your childhood is long gone . . .
I see my soon-to-be rabbi is done writing,
looking to share, tell . . . I cage my panic, peek from
the darkness engulfing me. I open myself to her,

to curiosity, listening. I have no answer, no way
toward an answer, no words at all. The question
haunts me, menaces, reverberates, snaps at my heels.
And then I recall, yes, there are moments when safety

descends—on the porch, allowing myself to do nothing
but listen for the birds, enjoy the leafy wisteria,
or in my study, just breathing, staring out the window,
watching the trees bud or the snow fall.

III

Ein Gedi

Shabbos together

The first time we made Shabbos together
in our own home—it wasn't really "our home,"
it was your third-floor walk-up and we weren't
even engaged yet. I had cooked chicken, my first
chicken, with a whole bulb of garlic—a clove?
a bulb? who knew?—my mother never used garlic.
And we sat down at that secondhand chrome table
in the kitchen. It was all so ugly that we turned out
the lights. Only the Shabbos candles flickered.

And then you made *kiddush*.

I sat there and wept—
Oh God, you have been so good to me!
Finally, for the first time in my life,
you gave me something I wanted.
This man, whose soul is the soul of Ein Gedi.
We will be silent together, we will open
our flowers in each other's presence.

And indeed we have bloomed through the years.

Stretching infinitely

We're living at the edge of the cornfields,
a girl from Brooklyn, a boy who grew up
on the Lower East Side, playing chess
in Tompkins Square Park. Kids who knew
the subway—14, 34, 42, 72, 96, 125.

Many bright young Easterners, newly minted
academics in their first position, band together
to bemoan missing bagels, mountains, seascapes,
but I fall in love with the open Midwestern vistas,
the flat plains which stretch infinitely.

I love the landscape of the sky, endless,
the ever-moving ever-changing sky—
theatrical to my eye. I love it most
in winter, watching sky stories unfold.
We go for Sunday drives, rural roads through
snow-covered cornfields. Explorers together.

Red enamel chairs

Our first real home, a duplex apartment at the edge
of the cornfields in a new development that boasts
a communal laundry room and a communal pool.
The small kitchen is separated from the dining area
by swinging café doors, and when guests compliment
the dinner, I call into the kitchen, *They liked it!*

Our furniture, a bizarre mix. Canopy bed, dresser,
armoire from a fancy Manhattan emporium—a gift
from his parents. Red bricks and boards configured into
bookcases and a coffee table. An old oak rocker we
spent a year stripping. Secondhand wood chairs I painted
bright red enamel. Ubiquitous posters of the '60s.

The first day he set out to work, I sat alone in that duplex
apartment, looking at the bright red enamel chairs,
cornfields out the window, feeling for all the world like
Katharine Ross, the final scene of *The Graduate*, the back
of the bus in her wedding gown next to Dustin Hoffman—
we've escaped. And what now. And who am I.

Our demons

When we fought, I could feel the tearing of love,
its belly ripped open, its tenderness exposed.
At the beginning and for many more years
we didn't even understand what the fights
were about. At the beginning, any tiny spark
could ignite, for instance, housekeeping matters,

like my ingenious innovative vacuuming method.
Every few weeks when you can clearly see numerous
dust balls, move them along the baseboard with the side
of your foot and then deep satisfaction to pick up
a large clump, in the final corner, with your hands.
Lillian would have been horrified, she dusted daily.

This made him burn and he kept asking me to hire
someone, but I refused, *We can't afford that*, code for
I don't want to clean myself but would be ashamed to pay.
I on the other hand cared about neat, a serene order
to every room, a balm to the eye. So when he never put
anything back where it belonged, my temper flared.

Fierce warriors, screaming, my tears, his closed doors.
Over and again, irreparable destruction of our world.
I brought anger as my dowry, he betrothed me in silence.
Later, battles over money, schools for the kids, in-laws.
He needed time for lucid thinking, not to be crowded,
pushed; I refused to be pliant, silenced like my mother.

Though we fought with sound and fury, there were lines
of respect we never crossed, and the will to survive
together was strongest of all. After a while, one would

reach a hand to the other, pulling the beloved up from
the primal reenacted darkness of childhood wounds,
into the light of softened eyes and willingness to hear.

At the bottom of a colorless world
for Laura

I started by staining lightly in the morning, then persistently
throughout the day. I took it easy, and then by evening
I took to my bed, called Fraser Lewis. It was Christmas night—
did he call back himself, or was it a junior person
on his service? No matter, the advice was to rest, so I did.

Eddie pulled a chair up to my side of the bed and read,
some short fiction by a woman of a bygone era—Dorothy Parker?
The writing, the characters, held my attention, though most of all
it was Eddie's voice that held me. Was there pain yet, cramping?
What I recall was the terror of a suddenly untrustworthy body.

Around midnight maybe, the staining had turned to bleeding,
so we went to the ER. There must have been pain by then
because I was lying on my side, holding myself, and turned
on my back with great reluctance for the on-call to examine me.
Involuntarily it seemed, words escaped from his mouth—

Oh my God! I don't think I asked why those were his words,
I was too frightened to ask. He said, *We'll keep you overnight.*
By then I was writhing, sweating profusely. They offered me
pain meds but I asked if the baby might still be okay, and they said,
Yes, maybe. So I refused to take anything that could cause her

harm. Only writing this now do I realize I was imagining
a girl . . . I labored all night. In agony, too naïve to understand
I was in labor, refusing anything for the pain, irrationally
hoping that my baby would survive, praying, trying to hold on
to her. By morning, spent, drenched in sweat, but somehow

surprisingly myself again, I got up to go to the bathroom
and sitting there on the toilet, I passed her out with my pee

and my blood. I looked at the bottom of the bowl, a mysterious
perfect rounded mass of tissue. I pulled the cord on the wall
for help. I asked the nurse, *Was that my baby?* And she said,

Perhaps. We'll have to see, fishing it out, whisking it away.
Was it possible I knew more than she, or was she protecting
herself from delivering bad news? All of this in a double room,
on the other side of the curtain a new mother, her baby,
colorful balloons and ecstatic visitors who clamored in to coo.

I've never been able to account for the months that followed—
January, February, March . . . It was cold and gray. I drifted.
I sank to the bottom of a colorless world, a woman without
a mother, a woman without a child. I had been mysteriously
deposited in a place so isolated, so set apart, no one could reach

me, touch me. Alone in the limitless gray, without horizons.

—December 25, 1976

When you come to it, you will not care
for Lisa and for her namesake, Lillian

Forty years ago today I lived in a young woman's body.
I see myself getting out of a car on a crisp late autumn
morning, 9 a.m. I see myself with a big belly, taut like a drum.
I am walking slowly toward the hospital doors, pausing
for contractions.

I'm hoping to get the brand-new birthing room with the pretty
Laura Ashley–like floral curtains. This is my first. My friend
Laura, who has had three, with a fourth on the way, enjoys
laughing at me about this—*Believe me, when you come to it,
you will not care!* Well, now I've come to it, and quite soon
I do not care.

I'm doing it the natural way, Eddie and I have been schooled
in Lamaze, I want to be awake to take in this miracle. Hours later,
I am stuck at seven centimeters, can't seem to get past seven.
Then the nurse on the next shift declares me to be only at six—
oh my God, no—going backwards?

Not possible! Then transition and I'm glaring at Eddie to *shut
the fuck up* as he tries to encourage me. Finally, time to push.
I feel like my insides are ripping apart. No contacts, no glasses,
in the end I can't see anything that's happening—eternal
regret. But finally, the baby, she's out, moving, crying,
they put her on my belly.

She latches on, she's nursing, she knows what to do.
This tiny hungry creature, startlingly strong, sucking hard
at my breast. She knows what to do. And I, I am crying,
crying, shaking, delirious, bathed in sweat, delirious

with pain and fear, releasing from pain and fear, delirious with joy. As I hold her, as she nurses, I keep repeating, *I wanted a girl, I wanted a girl.*

—NOVEMBER 21, 1978, 3:26 P.M.

Coming of age
for Uri

A glorious June day, I'm on the porch reading,
and my son carries a large black Hefty bag
out of the house, out to the garbage,
the muscles of his upper arms straining.

A college graduate for five days now,
living at home with us for one last summer,
he's cleaning his room, discarding emblems
of childhood to make way for the man he is
becoming. But I am the daughter of Depression

parents, and I wonder what is in that Hefty bag,
wonder if a son born of this disposable culture
can make an imaginative leap to Salvation Army
and hand-me-downs, wonder if that Hefty bag
holds anything of value that could be handed down.

I wonder, but understand that pawing through
his garbage is not an option: what is required of me
is patience and respect, a leap of faith,
the capacity to live with uncertainty.

IV

Lillian

The straw, day one

What I remember most clearly, what I've never been able
to forget, is the straw. It was late at night,
the room was dimly lit, we came straight
from the airport. She was lying in bed
and the nurse had a cup of water
and a straw.

Delicately, knowingly, she dipped the straw into the cup,
closed her finger over the top to create a vacuum,
then slowly released a few drops at a time
with the straw to my mother's lips,
to moisten them, to provide
relief.

The watch, day two

The next morning I noticed he was wearing
her watch. The thinnest elastic faux gold wristband,
the tiny face—how many scores of those watches
had she bought and worn over a lifetime?
It looked ridiculous on his thick wrist.
I guess he put it on when they admitted her,
to keep track of it, to feel connected.

The doctor arrives. He pronounces a harsh
and senseless ruling—we may each see her
for no more than ten minutes, twice a day.
Mini-visits, set apart, one at a time.
He *doesn't want to tire her out.* She's
dying, I think, we've come all this way
for a touch, a word, to sit with her
in silence, anything—*tire her out?*

But this is long ago and he is the doctor
and I am the youngest of all, so young,
unpracticed at dealing with doctors,
unpracticed at dying. Eddie questions,
no one else protests, I say nothing.

The waiting room, day two

We sit together in the waiting room, uncomfortably
together. She was the one who held us
together, and now her power to hold is finished.
Four of us, and Eddie—Eddie is apart, here by virtue
of being mine, but an adjunct, with privileges.

The men in my family do not speak, except
of course, with teasing, jokes. Or anger, cruelty.
And there is clearly no place here in the waiting
room for any of that. One by one, we take
our turn, our pathetic ten-minute turns.

Eddie reports she asked him to read to her,
some psalms. He does, but is nervously eyeing
his watch. Ten minutes turn to thirteen. He fears
she thinks he wants to flee—she sees him
checking his watch. Torn, he stretches the minutes,

but then finally, must go. The memory haunts him—
how dearly he loved her. Like a mother.

What he knew, day two

Is it my imagination or is my father
not taking his turn? It's all so impossibly hard
to focus, to recall, but I think he keeps saying
to the four of us, *No, you go next.*

Lillian was the youngest—parents, siblings,
all gone. He, her high school sweetheart,
is her oldest living friend. She loved him
unwaveringly, through all the hardships,

much to our detriment in fact. She didn't know
how to stop giving love—against her nature.
But then, these last years, alone together,
sunny Florida, she seemed finally to see him

with clarity, finally to see the selfishness,
his profoundly crippled soul. I suspect,
in the end, she didn't want him, and he knew.

What was he thinking, sitting in the waiting room.

The dance card

Fewer and fewer people know what it means
when I say, "My dance card is full." Yet another
anachronism I enjoy explaining. In olden times,
when a girl went to a dance, a ball, she had a small
card with a slim pencil attached by a braided cord

and if a boy wanted to dance with her, he approached
and asked to write his name on her card, assuring him
the pleasure of a waltz or a foxtrot. (Origin of foxtrot—
vaudeville term, circa 1914.) In any case, sitting in my study
in Western Massachusetts, I'm holding in my hands

my mother's dance card, dated Monday, June 27, 1927.
On the cover is printed in a very fancy font *E.D.H.S.*—
Eastern District High School. Opening the card, I see
at the bottom, credit for the music attributed to
Sid's Hotsy Totsy Orchestra. Two facing columns

each listing six dances, a mix of foxtrots and waltzes,
and a line on which a boy could sign. My mother's
card was full, a phalanx of boys—Morris Kaplan (2),
Jacob Schlefer, Paul Weber, Ed Joseph, Harry, Sig,
Schrier, J.H.G., and three dances promised to Milt.

Milt, the one she would marry, Milt, the one
who won her heart, Milt, the one she loved, Milt,
the one who brought her years of joy before he
didn't. On the back of the card, class officers are listed—
we discover Lillian Uhrbach was class Sec'y. Also

on the back is written in pencil an enigmatic
question—*Wanna buy a watch?* And below, perhaps
in the same hand, *O.K. see you later.* Indispensable

Google suggests possible link to Groucho Marx routine,
but really, the exchange remains a mystery.

What must you have looked like at that dance,
in a dress you sketched from a storefront display
that your mother then sewed. A slip of a girl, sixteen,
your small lithe body, graceful, full of spirit, joy,
commanding a phalanx of boys, waiting for their dance.

The day the marriage ended

They couldn't see it, but
the first time he ordered the boy,
Pull down your pants
and she didn't put her body
between the man and the boy—
that was the day the marriage
ended.

The boy was the first fruit
of their love. Together they
adored him, bathed him,
fed him, played with him,
read to him, put aside pennies
to buy him toys and little
treats.

But baby cheeks and dimples
morphed into adolescent angles
and gawkiness, the boy gingerly
took a few small steps
to independence, the mildest
disobedience, while the man's fortunes
fell.

All the heartbreak of repeated missed
opportunities, bitter disappointment,
ambition thwarted, failure—broke
his manly sweetness. Playfulness
replaced by rigid pride, need for control.
He took off his belt and let loose
rage.

And she, always a wisp of a girl,
brimming with love, adoration

for this tall dark charmer, she couldn't
bring herself, couldn't imagine,
crossing him, challenging him,
going up against him, telling him
No.

In that instant, rage flaring in his nostrils,
violence in his forearms, thick hands,
his belt tearing the boy's flesh, he became
someone new, crossed over to someone
new, a soul separated from itself,
secret shame. The marriage, the family,
lost.

The very end of day two

After we'd all had supper together, I wanted to see her, 10 minutes
be damned. Back to the hospital, an illicit visit, under cover of darkness.
In the dimly lit room, she was awake, seemed more present, peaceful.
I had announced hours earlier that I was pregnant—how she had longed
for that, waited. Now she looked at me sidewise, quizzically, wondering,
doubting, she asked, *Really? Did I dream it? Did you say that because
I'm dying?* I reassure, *Truly, Mom. Really.*

It was so early, I wouldn't have told, but under the circumstances. Sitting
by her bed, I realized I had a question—*Tell me about the day I was born.*

*It was such a beautiful autumn day, crisp, clear,
the leaves turning, brisk morning chill. I called
Dr. Rubenstein—he lived across the street—
and I said, "I'm in labor, I'll be walking over to
the hospital now." He was so upset. He just wouldn't
have it—he insisted on driving me. I was sorry really.
It was such a beautiful morning, and I love to walk.*

Then she turned on her side and said, *I'm very tired now,*
and those were the last words she spoke.
A month later, at twelve weeks, I lost that baby.

Day three becomes day four

We arrive at the hospital, day three. The doctor
says she's in a coma. Now we can sit with her.

I had no idea people in a coma can hear—did anyone
know that, back then? We held her hand, we wandered
in and out, we talked about the funeral and where to sit shivah,
we talked about *narishkeit*. We wondered aloud how long
a coma might last . . . Day three becomes day four.

An orderly brings in a breakfast tray—absurd enough,
but on the tray, a paper foldout turkey—Thanksgiving.

Had I realized she was still there, still listening, what I would have
softly whispered, what I would have sung, how I would have
stroked her face, kissed her, held her close. I do remember though
I called her *Lillian*, I reasoned she was more *Lillian* than *Mom*.
I thought, wouldn't that be the name she wanted at the end?

At 12:30 her breathing stopped, and then I sang—
Pitchu li, shaarei tzedek, avo vam odeh Yah—Open
for her the gates of the righteous so she may enter.

        —THANKSGIVING DAY, NOVEMBER 25, 1976

V

Temporarily, unexpectedly

When they're gone, do people know that they're remembered?
for Max and Esther Ticktin

A newlywed, I'm living in the Midwest, Champaign-Urbana—
flat flat but I don't mind, I love the sky. We've driven up
to Chicago, visiting with Eddie's esteemed colleague and his wife.
I am very young, a guest, new to all of this, even to being a guest,
and I'm asked what I'd like for breakfast. Too shy to declare myself,
I want to be wallpaper. The negotiations proceed—*eggs? cereal?
juice?* Slowly getting the gist of my predicament, they playfully
maneuver me into saying, *Just a roll and butter please.*

Then they all burst out in loving laughter and tell me Peretz's
story of Bontshe Shvayg. Bontshe the Silent, silent through
unending torments all his life. Finally, before the Heavenly Court,
he is offered a reward beyond imagining—*Whatever you want,
everything is yours*, the Judge declares. But after a lifetime
of neglect, mockery, scorn, infidelity, derision, Bontshe is beyond
asking or even imagining—*Just a roll and butter please.*

Max and Esther, learned Yiddishists both, explain how this captures
the iconic Jewish dilemma—is Bontshe holy for allowing himself
to be invisible? Or is he a cautionary tale, sinful even, for not having
grabbed hold of life, imagined, made demands? My young eyes
widen—what world is this? who ever imagined such a breakfast,
sitting at a table, talking like this, at breakfast? Did I see then

that I was Bontshe? Did they? Max and Esther, my first adult friends.
With their insatiable curiosity, intelligence, kindness, they encouraged,
inspired, dared me—to ask, to imagine, demand. In my memories
they live, continue to surprise, each memory an unfolding, a random
roll with butter and a thousand memories more—each memory
a proof text for blessing the One who resurrects the dead.

His many foreign lands
for our teacher, Reb Zalman, 1924–2014

Oh Zalman, how I missed you this Shabbos, remembering a bit
of psalm you put to unlikely country-western music and sang
in English. Round and round I repeated the well-known words,
the lifting notes . . . *If I forget thee, Jerusalem, let me forget my right
hand, if I forget thee, Jerusalem, let me forget my right hand.*

How can I sing the praise of the Lord, in a foreign land?
If I forget thee, Jerusalem, let me forget my right hand.

1968 Boston, the first *havurah*—pillows on the floor,
we rocked and davened. I, the youngest, true beginner's mind,
you, the oldest, a sage, a guru, practicing *tzimtzum*. You,
exploding with wonder, joy, unimaginable fertility,
your Eastern European davening in English a revelation

in which I heard a secret message—*it's all right,*
Merle, you're good enough, God knows English too.

The next year you came to visit us, living on the edge
of the cornfields. It was spring, our newlywed home
a brick and board extravaganza—bookcases, tables.
In your pack, always full of marvels, a knife sharpener.
I never travel without it, you said, and asked for our knives,

explaining, *I figure, if the rabbinate doesn't work out,*
I can always go town to town, sharpening knives.

Saturday night, the four of us played Monopoly,
a Mad Hatter's version—the triumph of socialism,
unapologetic, unselfconscious. *Malka, if I give you my*
Marvin Gardens you'll have the yellows. I can loan
you the money to build houses, or maybe build hotels?

Did you not understand the premise of a competitive game,
or was it just too much fun disrupting a greedy world order?

The last time, fifty years later, full circle in Boston, Kraindel's
birthday, you greeted me with sweet love, *Merle beautiful poet!*
Unsure, I wondered—beautiful me? poetry? both? Precious,
that davening, looking around the room, breathing all together.
How can I sing the praise of the Lord in a foreign land?

Yesterday I remembered your stories from after Vienna—
rescued by the Rebbe's family, youthful travels, an emissary
for Chabad, *shechting* chickens, welcoming new baby boys.
An itinerant in so many foreign lands. But I never heard a story
from before, from Vienna before, the world you lost. Where
did you keep those stories, Zalman, where did you keep that pain,
in your holy colliding of worlds, so many foreign lands?

Aunt Julie's final conversation

My Aunt Julie, a truly good simple woman, married late.
I have no idea what went on inside that shabby small apartment,
but whenever I saw him, her husband was gruff, short-tempered.
Too early—in her late fifties—she became more confused
than usual, forgetting words, laughing more and more inappropriately,
wandering the neighborhood in her housedress or worse, lost,
inviting strange people up to the apartment. A diagnosis,
and then she was living in a special wing of the same old-age
home where her mother was living and making new friends
in her eighties, crocheting blankets with her gnarled hands.

Grandma died first, Julie lingered another few years, repeating
two words in a conversational tone with the shining smile
we knew so well—*temporarily, unexpectedly*—over and over
that was the extent of her conversation. Of course, everyone
wondered—why those two words. The home had rabbis who
officiated when the time came; by chance, I knew the one
who led her graveside funeral, Nathan Goldberg, a good man.
And by a stroke of stunning insight or deep spiritual acumen, he
centered the simple eulogy on those two words, imagining her life's
final *d'rash*—*We are here temporarily; unexpectedly, we disappear.*

What courage looks like
for Elana

Long ago you were suffering—a cloud dense
and wide and deep had settled over you, choking out
light, pleasure, ease. You had lost yourself in a place
faraway, too far to be reached, to be touched,
numb, paralyzed by pain, alone. Unable to drive,

you came on a train and I picked you up at the station.
A New England autumn day, my backyard a carpet of
vibrant God-filled colors, leaves twirling, falling.
The air was crisp, our cheeks ruddy. I had two rakes,
and we spent a few hours that afternoon raking.

Maybe we talked—yes, now I remember—we did talk,
and I made lunch. Over many months you came back
to yourself, and every few years, one of us reminds
the other of the leaves, the afternoon of raking.
Since I still live in the same house, same backyard, trees,

every autumn as the leaves display their glory
and fall, I look out my kitchen window and I see
the two of us raking leaves. I marvel that, along with many,
I and the leaves were able to help. More though, I marvel
at your courage, holding on to life and opening to me.

You offer me full-throated laughter
for JM, 1940–2016

You are delicate like the irises you favor, you aspire to a world stage.
And though you sometimes play fast and loose with the truth, a quality
I do not normally abide in friends, nonetheless I offer you my loyalty,
indeed, a place in my dearest inner circle. What opens my heart
is your vulnerability that seeks protection. You come to my kitchen
always hungry, grateful to sit and talk while I bake my Friday challahs
and feed you your favorite cheeses and homemade bagels. A waif,
you feel safe in my kitchen, and it is my pleasure to offer you safety.

I intertwine my years with yours, you rely on me to listen, to care,
and giving boundless love binds me all the closer. We share the same
uncanny gifts for generosity and gentle listening, without judgment.
We keep each other's secrets. You offer unparalleled, irreplaceable
full-throated laughter, your forte is fun—an appetite, a knowledge
of pleasure. Walks on winter beaches and winding Parisian side streets,
the latest movie and the classics, off-Broadway, the great museums
and small little-known jewels overflowing with Impressionists.

Together we enjoy well-told stories, fine chocolate. The waiters blink
in disbelief when you, size 2, order your second sundae, espresso
ice cream with extra real whipped cream on the side. You know,
it is your pleasure, to draw me into pleasure, adventure. And then,
unexpectedly, a diagnosis—the long goodbye, disappearing from
yourself. You cannot face it, refuse, will not be persuaded to linger.
You make your arrangements and I visit for a last week together;
leaving, I offer to accompany you on the phone the final morning.

Me, in my flannel pajamas, wrapped against nasty New England
March chill, waiting for your call. You in your sunny bedroom,
impeccable, hair coiffed, full makeup, delicate lace peignoir.
Your first words—*I'm not afraid and I'm not changing my mind.*

Already having said everything, we sing together—Cole Porter, the Broadway show tunes of our youth, a little Dylan too. One hundred minutes later, it is time—*they'll be here any minute.*

We say goodbye.

The pain of your loss
for Jane Trigere, 1948–2018

Lady Jane, with your exquisitely chiseled
features, unending curiosity, your sly
delicious wit, wide streak of stubbornness,
and the sharp cactus prickle guarding
luminosity within—wanting

to love, wanting to be loved, wanting
so much. With your myriad gifts—
of hand, of eye, of heart, imagination,
intelligence—with your outrageously
abundant gifts, you could never

have achieved all your dreams—
your dreams and your gifts
were without limit. Lately I declare
my truth to friends, *If I lived to 120,
I would not have exhausted*

all my ideas of what to create.
Jane, my sister, that was you.
In the end, Jane, I hope you were
at peace with the life you had lived,
pleased with all you had created.

I found many helpful words for you
while you were alive, but found
these last particular words only now,
too late. I hope somehow in the end
you knew. You knew, after all, so much.

The pain of your loss is quite raw.
I have barely begun to cry.

I'm not finished talking
and I'm not finished
listening.
>   —*Lady Merle*

VI

Not even on the way anywhere

The story of how we came to Western Mass

How broken I was when we left New York, fleeing the prestigious
gig that had courted us to come, then used us, abused us, poisoned
the very air in our home, poisoned even Shabbos. My sweet daughter
imperiled, my son's belief in goodness shaken, the marriage
in tatters. A new job offered reprieve, escape, faint hope.

On the cusp of that change, Roger died. In March, an out-of-
nowhere ER call—pancreatic cancer. Vigorous health, playing
tennis, golf—gone. In April he was dead. All the conversations
I'd waited to have, years' worth of slowly unfolding questions,
impossible now. Instead, eternally unanswerable questions. Pain

everywhere, unending. June and July, I emptied his condo,
getting it ready for sale: piles for Goodwill, for trash, sentimental
piles for family and friends, carefully wrapping and mailing
across the country the heavy pottery he'd made, bequeathing
something to remember him by. Going through his things,

multiple discoveries—a delicate balancing toy I bought him
in high school when I worked in the Brooklyn Museum Gallery Shop,
a brick from when they tore down Ebbetts Field—his love for the Dodgers
fierce. And in a drawer of this well-to-do corporate consultant, many
pairs of darned socks, along with the wooden egg Grandma had used.

All in a tumble then, we sold our West End Avenue apartment,
put his condo up for sale, searched for a house and a high school
in Western Mass, packed another child off to college. I quickly filled
a fat notebook with this dizzying number of projects, each with its own
section, notes, names, phone numbers—I'm very well organized.

We bought this house and moved, three months after getting up
from shivah. I unpacked around the clock until every book, chair,
mug had found its proper place. And then I rolled up the sidewalk,
crawled into bed. Thanksgiving weekend I broke my ankle, which
provided me the perfect excuse to officially become a recluse.

Only at the deliberate pace of someone in rehab learning to walk
again did I begin to regain myself. Credit for that goes to Leighton
and to this house. Deep in my soul, in my belly and shoulders,
I began to feel at home. First, I settled into the welcoming wraparound
porch with its aged lush wisteria, offering shade in late afternoon,

privacy from passersby, but also a view out to the street for observation.
I came to love the entry hall's thick oak banister, the feel of it in my hand,
the wood so solid and true, trustworthy. I enjoyed the gracious proportions
and flow of the rooms, the old oak floors, the living room with a bit
of leaded glass and a window seat that hides toys and books to surprise

young visitors. An eat-in kitchen. And a fireplace—I ached for that,
insisted on that—I needed hypnotic crackling flames to soothe, comfort,
stare at vacantly, not thinking at all . . . Later, the little front yard garden
planted slowly over years. Of course, in early spring, tulips and daffodils;
then day lilies and tiger lilies and black-eyed Susans, lavender and daisies,

mums, and my favorites, though I know one shouldn't have favorites—
huge Oriental red poppies with their dramatic black stamens, presiding
far too briefly over all, stopping in their tracks strollers and dog walkers,
who ask permission to take pictures, or just silently worship, paying
tribute to the poppy's beauty proclaiming the glory of God.

January 9, 2017
anticipating Inauguration

This month in my small New England town
fifty refugees will begin to arrive from Syria, Iraq,
Burundi, the Democratic Republic of Congo.
The local paper reports that seven hundred volunteers
have stepped forward to help welcome them,
to provide apartments, houses, bedding and pots,
diapers and spoons, tissues, toys, shoes, winter
coats, trips to the supermarket and to doctors,
job leads and English classes for a new start.

Seven hundred strong we will share with these strangers
all we can imagine they need to make a new life, safe.

The need of the strangers is great, and we are eager
to welcome, to help, to give, to share. Excited
as children, we await the as-yet-undetermined date
of their arrival. Unspoken is the truth that while our
needs are puny compared to theirs, still our need
for them is great. We ache to embody the good we believed
was our country's ideal, we ache to hold onto some tiny
shard of the pride we felt as children pledging allegiance,
singing, *O say can you see*.

We await their arrival with our broken hearts, all the while
bracing ourselves, gathering courage for the Unimaginable.

Icy listserv mornings

The snowy icy mornings blur into one another.
The cold is bitter, penetrating bones, an angry
climate is punishing us all, though other parts
of the country and other worlds are suffering more.
On one of those mornings this month, a woman

whose name I don't know reaches out on the listserv—
*My partner is away, I'm alone in the house. I have
a fever and need some Tylenol and juice. Is anyone
going shopping, could you add on a few things for me?*
I read this maybe five minutes after it was sent,

respond at once—*What's your address? We're
not plowed yet but could just walk over.* She
sends a second message—*Problem already
solved, I am overwhelmed by all your responses.*
And, cc'ing all, I write back to her—*Thank you!*

We've all found ourselves in the house, sick
and alone, but whoever thought to reach out like this
for help? Now we all know, help is right here,
on the next block, whether you know me or not.
Everyone feels less afraid.

Working from home

Sometimes we meet on the phone and sometimes
we Skype, we Zoom. I wait for the call, prepped with B's
or L's or Z's file, the notes I have taken as they talk
and I listen. My clients are rabbis, some cantors, some
students on their way to becoming, though truly, each
and all of them are on their way to becoming, as am I.
I ask questions, a freedom forbidden me in childhood.

S writes, then she reads, I listen, we talk. And then
the next question . . . J keeps opening—writing, talking,
opening. I trust my instincts to find the questions
they need, like clues in a treasure hunt. Together we mine
stories, the quickening pulse they've noticed in the writing—
his sorrow after three funerals in a row, her pain at
immigrant travesties, his delight in new fatherhood,

her stunning High Holiday sermon. The missteps, the triumphs,
the confusion—we mine it all, the days, the long minutes,
again and again, questions, writing, opening doors. When they
are afraid, I help them see how strong they are, how competent.
Sometimes we look at what went wrong, what can be learned,
gleaned. When they have found a steady resting place, feel
refreshed and reinforced, I gently challenge them to open

the next beckoning door. They think me wise, though really,
I introduce them to their own wisdom. My elevator speech?
Educational consultant—the shorthand is easy, true in its way.
How did I learn to do this? From those who have listened well
to me, embodied listening. Why do I do this? I discovered my gift
for offering safety to others, the deep satisfaction of that, the peace.
Something I could never offer Warren.

What's your emergency?
for Margaret

Our neighborhood listserv announces rallies, concerts, updates on
the woman in sanctuary at the local church; queries for snow
removal, dentists; offers of free furniture, a used printer, old dishes.
At 8:45 the morning after Thanksgiving, I open my email to discover
we are waking up to an unfolding crisis. Beth has spotted forty geese
on Paradise Pond, seemingly frozen to the ice, wildly flapping wings
but going nowhere.

She's tried campus police but they don't know what to do. Claire posts,
Call Cummington Wildlife. I for my part call 911—*What's your
emergency?* asks the on-duty. *I know this isn't an emergency, but
there are fifty geese on Paradise Pond freezing to death—who do I call?*
Quickly they transfer me and the next voice says, *Animal Control—
I'm on it*. Sarah reports back with numerous FB sites. Meanwhile,
a human chain is forming.

Cindy and her daughter heading there to help, call Mass Wildlife
and think they will need paddleboards and kayaks to get to where
you can chop the ice. Rachel: *There was a news crew filming
at 10:30 when I went by for my morning run*. Cindy reports back,
*Now there are over a hundred geese here, police and fire department,
really nice campus police*. They play a "hawk and eagle" call,
a few geese start to walk around.

All decide the geese are fine, remain to caution from going out
on the ice. At 11:20, as some of us are thinking which leftovers
to serve up for lunch, Frannie posts what her online research
has revealed: *Geese have a unique circulation system in their feet.
Their feet can't freeze. They often sleep on top of ice in lakes.*

When we moved to Western Mass in 1996, my oldest friend,
a proud lifelong New Yorker, quipped, *Northampton?! It's
not even on the way anywhere!*

VII

Then laughed and laughed, ageless

Solstice

Lying in bed,
our limbs intertwined,
anchored and warm under old down,
the night sky still dark
and suddenly, my blood stops.
I can feel the platelets piling up
in the pause, the wave's crest
higher and higher, unnatural—
can blood flow backwards?
And I recognize
my body has turned to fear,
fear in the blood, in the platelets,
waking me, with no memory
of dreaming.

The enemy is time.

Jane is explaining

why she committed to her highly disciplined
food program and how she lost forty pounds
in five months and has been able to keep it off.

I no longer recognized myself in the mirror,
she says. She wants me to do this too,
she's unhappy and dissatisfied when I tell her,

I've been cutting out almost all sugar—it inflames
my arthritis and will cripple me. *What do you
mean by "almost all"?* she challenges triumphantly,

as if catching me in an illogical trap. *You need
the program to do it right.* I love how we both
in our own ways are so sure of what we are sure of.

Jane is a beautiful woman, a regal bearing.
I can imagine her, in her prime, wearing elegant
clothes, designing and sewing for a proud ripe body.

She's dying now, I don't like to contradict her,
so I wait till the diatribe is spent and then
say mildly, sideways, *I never recognized*

myself in the mirror. In fact, growing up,
we had only two small mirrors—how old
was I until I saw myself, all, at once?

What I don't say is that mostly I'm ambivalent
about losing weight. When the scale dips I feel
fear, dread—how can I both reveal myself

and remain safe in the world? Jane is tired now,
drifting off, chemo has taken a lot out of her.
We'll talk again tomorrow.

A bell rings

The realization, as slow, lazy, innocent as a wave
lapping the shore of a country lake—I become aware
that my tongue is numb, thick, lazy. Uncooperative,
as if shot through with Novocain, as if it's gone to sleep.
And my lips, my mouth are numb. In the mirror my face
looks funny, lopsided. I can grimace all the way up
into my left cheek, but the right side is going nowhere.

I want to keep my appointments. I have a strong stubborn
will—I will will myself to be okay. But fear in the blood,
in the platelets, overcomes denial, wishful thinking. In the car,
the passenger seat, I cancel appointments, leave messages.
Why is this happening, what is happening, this can't be happening,
didn't I will it not to happen—I have a strong will. How many
appointments will I have to cancel, how long will this take?

I approach the admitting desk, shaking, inside begging, *Help me
please*. The ER doctor with the strange name—he's good, I know
him—makes many strange faces at me, asks me to mimic, asks me
to do the outstretched arms. He's especially interested that my left
brow arches high up while the right stays put. *We need a CT scan
to be sure, but I don't think this is a stroke, I think it's Bell's palsy.*
I cling to the strangeness of the name—better than a stroke, yes?

A few hours, blood tests and the like. Will my symptoms disappear
or is this the new me? Yes, the tests come back, it seems to be
Bell's palsy. I ask, *Does this recur?* Not clear. *Could it come back,
be worse? Could it lead to a stroke?* I'm asking good questions,
important questions, but the words of the answers feel far away,
indistinct. Prescription for prednisone. I don't like that, don't
want that, have heard a lot about that. But I seem to have no say.

The next day, at home, I come back to myself. Organized, I make
an elaborate chart—6 pills 2x/day for 5 days, then 5 pills 2x/day
for 1 day, then 4, 3, 2, 1. Another pill 3x/day for 7 days. The chart

gives me a sense, a small measure, of control. Next, I realize, I need
a way to talk about this. Do I say, *I had Bell's palsy?* or, *I have Bell's
palsy?* or maybe, *I had an incident, an occurrence, of Bell's palsy?*
I don't want to, but feel honor-bound to tell my children.

They will be upset but they are adults and they have a right to know—
when they are sick, I want to know—I count on their honesty,
don't I owe them the same? Deeper though is the need to say aloud
to someone, not them, what this means to me, what I am afraid of.
Will this come again? Will it be more severe? Will it disfigure me?
My smile looks all wrong, will it return as my smile, or will it
make people squirm, staring resolutely at their shoes?

And what if I do have a stroke, a bad one? Am I a person with the strength,
the courage, to relearn speech, movement? And what if my brain fries
and I really can't come back? Increasingly I feel, if I can't be here as me,
I don't want to be here. Would my family have the strength to let me go?
As I write now, fear is flooding me, I have such strong feelings about
"not being left like that." But it's all been theoretical so far—could it
become real? soon? Dress rehearsal rag.

Under a stone
Jacob moves away the stone for Rachel

In the morning
unable to rise
I remain under
the comforter,
confused,
somehow covered

as if by a stone,
my heart
barely flickering,
somehow covered,
under a stone.

I imagine myself
rising, but rising
seems far away,
some distant planet
I cannot touch.

I look at
the small book
I keep
within reach
on my night table
with dates

and times,
people and places.
I look to see
the first hour
when someone
awaits me,

the first hour
I have made
a promise.
A thin cord
attached to
that promise

pulls me
and I rise,
tentatively
finding the strength
to move away
the stone.

I cannot
break
a promise.

Respite after darkness

The rising joy in the morning
when I wake with little pain,
my spirit peacefully coming
to consciousness. I wake with
the rising light, warm
under comforter and rising
hissing steam.

Beside me I hear beloved
soft breathing. I have come
through the darkness intact.
I rise on new calf's legs,
wobble to the bathroom.

Blessed is the One who
returns me to my life, who
rises me back to my life.

Returning

Then tired, we went home
and made love. For the first time
in a long time. All the weight
I'd been carrying, the pain
and anguish, the terror, guilt,
the suffering, began to melt away,
to dissolve, lift. So by the time
we were touching, I felt free,
entitled to joy, pleasure, ready
to receive, and to give.

I cried a little, then laughed and laughed,
ageless.

Stay with me a little longer please
sitting again with the yahrzeit candle

When I was ten, afraid you'd leave me, you'd die, I asked,
and you responded, *I won't die till you don't need me anymore.*
And I believed you, I believed everything you said, even
when I knew it wasn't true—*Of course your father loves you,
he just has his own way of showing it.*

So I imagined there would come a time when I was almost
old, and you were very old, and that's when you would
leave me—"when I didn't need you anymore"—imagining
that when you're almost old, you wouldn't need a mother.
But none of it was true—he loathed me; you died

when I was still quite young and still needed you; and you need
a mother always. Through the full years and the parched years,
I've learned to find glimpses, moments of your love—
as I embody tenderness with my daughter, son, my dearest
friends, my students. I give a mother's love to many. Repeatedly,

I recreate the rhythm, the release, of mother and child, nursing.
And still I love you, even though regarding matters of the gravest
importance, you lied. Still, I miss the soft waves of your hair,
your generous smile, I miss touching you and your touch on me.
I miss the smell of you, the light that shone from you. I miss

your ready laugh, your sweetness, the sound of you singing.
Our world was a treacherous place and you couldn't even protect me
in our tiny apartment. Nonetheless, you loved me, and that
was enough. It gave me the strength to keep getting up, to go out,
to go on. It's one of your mysteries I am still unraveling.

Thank you for bringing me here.

The world we have longed for
since the very beginning
for Warren

Another day, I ask a young rabbi—*When do you feel safe?*
I am surprised by his answer. *I feel safe when I am seen.*
No, I think, not me. I return to this question, but again,
insight continues to elude me. Finally, in slow-motion,
an epiphany: the question demands a wider scope.

I look back over an adult life, moments, stories, images,
the private sphere, and work. I see myself making a home,
many years of faces glowing around my Shabbos table,
impressionable students, curious, watchful. By candlelight,
we talk, we sing, we sit in comfortable silence.

Teaching remedial writing, a community college adjunct.
Career Army, waitresses, retired cops, homemakers—
so full of shame at what they don't know.
I know shame. I see them, care about them and their stories,
comment on their papers in detail, with interest, respect.

In the first intifada, I am on the West Bank, accompanying
Palestinians and Israelis as they dare to be honest, vulnerable
with one another, to work at listening. Amidst anger, anguish,
the hardest thing—to break through suspicion, inherited hatreds,
to see the face of the other. Why me? Someone was needed.

An eleventh-century town in Belarus, with three generations
of Jewish women—I widen their view of prayer, welcome them
to their place at the table. In Kiev, Solomon University, I read poems
about love and ironing, wicked secrets of a feminist life.
A fiery-eyed young woman: *Stalin is turning over in his grave!*

At Seeds of Peace, a man in dialogue, out of control, threatening,
shaking, raging—I move to sit next to him, my hand on his back,

anchoring him, willing him with my hand to calm, soften, breathe.
I feel the violence of his shaking, I just keep my hand there,
and ever so slowly, he sees again possibilities.

Later, in Chicago, Portland, Palo Alto, in Miami, Maine,
Ohio, Georgia, I am reading my poems, painful and true,
reentering the feelings, afterwards leading deep conversation.
The truth of the poems has allowed space for courageous connection—
how we all ache to speak to one another in truth.

Mentoring rabbis, seasoned and new—from my hundred-year-old house,
in public spaces and in small rooms where I come bearing flowers,
a colorful cloth, a favorite hand-thrown mug—in these scenes and more,
wherever I sit and listen, I cast a circle—here you are safe,
no harm will come to you on my watch.

When do I feel safe? That question is too small for me—
it's not about my safety. I climb over my fears, they are not interesting.
I break rules, create rules—here cruelty is forbidden, here we trust,
respect, protect one another from harm. Here together we dare to make
the world we want to share, the world we have longed for
since the very beginning.

Glossary

Bar'chu: Hebrew; in Jewish liturgy, the call to prayer, recited publicly in the presence of a minyan of ten adult Jews; a point of contention for feminists when women are not counted as part of the minyan.

Bell's palsy: Type of temporary facial paralysis that results in an inability to control the facial muscles on the affected side. Symptoms can vary from mild to severe.

bensch: Yiddish; to recite the blessings after a meal; in this case, to lead such blessings publicly, an honor not permitted to women before this era.

bimah: Hebrew; podium or platform in a synagogue from which the prayer leader officiates and reads from Torah and Prophets.

Chabad (also known as Lubavitch): Chasidic movement, known especially for its outreach activities.

davening: Yiddish; praying.

d'rash/d'rashah: Hebrew; expansive interpretation or explication, especially of but not limited to biblical and other religious texts.

Ein Gedi: A particularly lush and beloved oasis in the Judean desert, sometimes a setting for Hebrew love poetry, first appearing in the Song of Songs.

havurah: Hebrew; small group of like-minded Jews who assemble for the purposes of facilitating Shabbat and holiday prayer services, sharing communal experiences such as life-cycle events, and Jewish learning. Often transliterated as *chavurah* but transliterated here to reflect the early groups in which the author was involved.

I won't let you go till you bless me: In Genesis 32:26, after wrestling in the night with a man/angelic being, Jacob insists, "I won't let you go till you bless me."

Kiddush: Hebrew; blessing over the wine that sanctifies the Sabbath or festival.

leyn: Yiddish; to chant from a Torah scroll, an honor not permitted to women before the present era.

"making Shabbos": To do the shopping, cooking, and cleaning necessary to prepare a home for the observance of the Sabbath, inaugurated by the lighting of Shabbos candles.

narishkeit: Yiddish; foolishness, nonsense, triviality.

"Not one, not two . . .": Complex prohibitions against counting Jews go back to biblical times; a traditional alternative is to count instead, "not one, not two . . ." when ascertaining if a minyan is present for prayer. For most of Jewish history, adult women present in the synagogue sat through this counting without being counted.

Peretz: Isaac Leib Peretz, best known as I. L. Peretz, 1852–1915, one of the great classical Yiddish language authors and playwrights from Poland.

Pittsburgh: Mass shooting at the synagogue Tree of Life–Or L'Simcha Congregation in the Squirrel Hill neighborhood of Pittsburgh on October 27, 2018, while Shabbat morning services were being held. Eleven people were killed and seven were injured.

Rabbi Sally Priesand (b. 1946): First woman rabbi ordained in America by a rabbinical seminary, and the second formally ordained woman rabbi in Jewish history, after Regina Jonas. Priesand was ordained by Hebrew Union College–Jewish Institute of Religion in June 1972.

the Rebbe: Rabbinic leader of a Chasidic sect; in this case it refers to the sixth Lubavitch dynastic leader, Yosef Yitzchak Schneersohn (1880–1950).

Seeds of Peace: Leadership development organization founded in 1993 whose main program brings youth and educators from areas of conflict around the world to its camp in Maine, providing experiences in conflict resolution and peace building.

shechting: Yiddish; kosher slaughtering of certain mammals and birds for food according to Jewish laws.

shivah: Hebrew; observance of the traditional Jewish laws of mourning, which include sitting on a lowered chair or stool for seven days.

Simchas Torah: Ashkenazi Hebrew pronunciation; Jewish holiday that marks and celebrates the conclusion of the annual cycle of public Torah readings and the beginning of the new cycle; typically observed by holding and dancing with the Torah scrolls. Until the current era, women were usually excluded from holding or dancing with the Torah. The pronunciation in Modern and Sephardic Hebrew is Simchat Torah.

Taamod: Hebrew; grammatical form for calling a woman up to the bimah for the honor of the Torah blessings (*aliyah laTorah*). For most of Jewish history, women were not permitted to be called to the Torah; the power of hearing this feminine form cannot be overestimated.

tzimtzum: Hebrew; concept from mystical kabbalistic Jewish thought and practice, here referring to a contraction of ego that gives others room to shine.

yahrzeit: Yiddish; anniversary of the death of a parent or close relative observed annually among Jews by the recital of the *Kaddish* memorial prayer and the lighting of a memorial candle.

Zalman: Zalman Schachter-Shalomi (1924–2014), raised in Vienna, escaped the Nazis in 1941, and subsequently was ordained as an Orthodox rabbi in the Chabad-Lubavitch Chasidic community. Zalman was a key founder of the Jewish Renewal Movement and impacted all of world Jewry through his extraordinary gifts as a teacher; his creativity, vitality, and unique ability to synthesize a vast range of traditional and contemporary forms have inspired generations.

Index of Titles

A bell rings, 75

At the bottom of a colorless world, 34

Aunt Julie's final conversation, 56

Coming of age, 38

Day three becomes day four, 50

He is gone for many hours, 7

His many foreign lands, 54

I keep his secrets, 9

I was the youngest, the only girl, 12

Icy listserv mornings, 68

In the corner, 3

Jane is explaining, 74

January 9, 2017, 67

Let my people go that we may serve You, vii

Mickey in the hallway, 17

My brother and I each separately, 4

Our demons, 32

Prospects, 22

Red enamel chairs, 31

Respite after darkness, 79

Returning, 80

Roger is the middle child, 11

Safe has disappeared, 6

Seder story, 8

Shabbos together, 29

Sixth-grade boys, 20

Sol by the pickle barrel, 15

Solstice, 73

Stay with me a little longer please, 81

Stretching infinitely, 30

The dance card, 45

The day the marriage ended, 47

The pain of your loss, 60

The story of how I started smoking, 23

The story of how we came to Western Mass, 65

The straw, day one, 41

The very end of day two, 49

The waiting room, day two, 43

The watch, day two, 42

The world we have longed for since the very beginning, 82

Under a stone, 77

What courage looks like, 57

What he knew, day two, 44

What makes you feel safe?, 25

What's your emergency?, 70

When they're gone, do people know that they're remembered?, 53

When you come to it, you will not care, 36

Working from home, 69

You offer me full-throated laughter, 58

About the Author

Photo: Edward Feld

MERLE FELD is an esteemed and beloved poet. She is the author of a memoir in poetry and prose—*A Spiritual Life: Exploring the Heart and Jewish Tradition*—and an earlier poetry collection, *Finding Words*. Her poems appear in a variety of groundbreaking volumes, including *Mishkan HaSeder, Mahzor Lev Shalem, Siddur Lev Shalem,* and *The Torah: A Women's Commentary*. Her award-winning plays *The Gates are Closing* and *Across the Jordan* have been presented nationally and internationally. Since 2000, she has been a pioneer in the field of spiritual writing, guiding rabbis, adult seekers, and clergy students across denominations to explore and deepen their spiritual lives (derekh.org). A recipient of honors for poetry, playwriting and activism, Merle has shared her life with Rabbi Edward Feld, a distinguished spiritual leader and author, with whom she has parented two children, Lisa and Uri.

CPSIA information can be obtained
at www.ICGtesting.com
Printed in the USA
BVHW051111250123
656982BV00012BA/1048

9 780881 236262